Math Counts

Counting

Introduction

In keeping with the major goals of the National Council of Teachers of Mathematics Curriculum and Evaluation Standards, children will become mathematical problem solvers, learn to communicate mathematically, and learn to reason mathematically by using the series Math Counts.

Pattern, Shape, and *Size* may be investigated first—in any sequence.

Sorting, Counting, and *Numbers* may be used next, followed by *Time, Length, Weight,* and *Capacity.*

Ramona G. Choos, Professor of Mathematics, Senior Adviser to the Dean of Continuing Education, Chicago State University; Sponsor for Chicago Elementary Teachers' Mathematics Club

About this Book

Mathematics is a part of a child's world. It is not only interpreting numbers or mastering tricks of addition or multiplication. Mathematics is about *ideas*. These ideas have been developed to explain particular qualities such as size, weight, and height, as well as relationships and comparisons. Yet all too often the important part that an understanding of mathematics will play in a child's development is forgotten or ignored.

Most adults can solve simple mathematical tasks without the need for counters, beads, or fingers. Young children find such abstractions almost impossible to master. They need to see, talk, touch, and experiment.

The photographs and text in these books have been chosen to encourage talk about topics that are essentially mathematical. By talking, the young reader can explore some of the central concepts that support mathematics. It is on an understanding of these concepts that a child's future mastery of mathematics will be built.

Henry Pluckrose

1995 Childrens Press® Edition
© 1994 Watts Books, London, New York, Sydney
All rights reserved.
Printed in China.
Published simultaneously in Canada.

14 15 16 17 18 R 14 13 12

Math Counts

Counting

By Henry Pluckrose

Mathematics Consultant: Ramona G. Choos,
Professor of Mathematics

 CHILDRENS PRESS®
CHICAGO

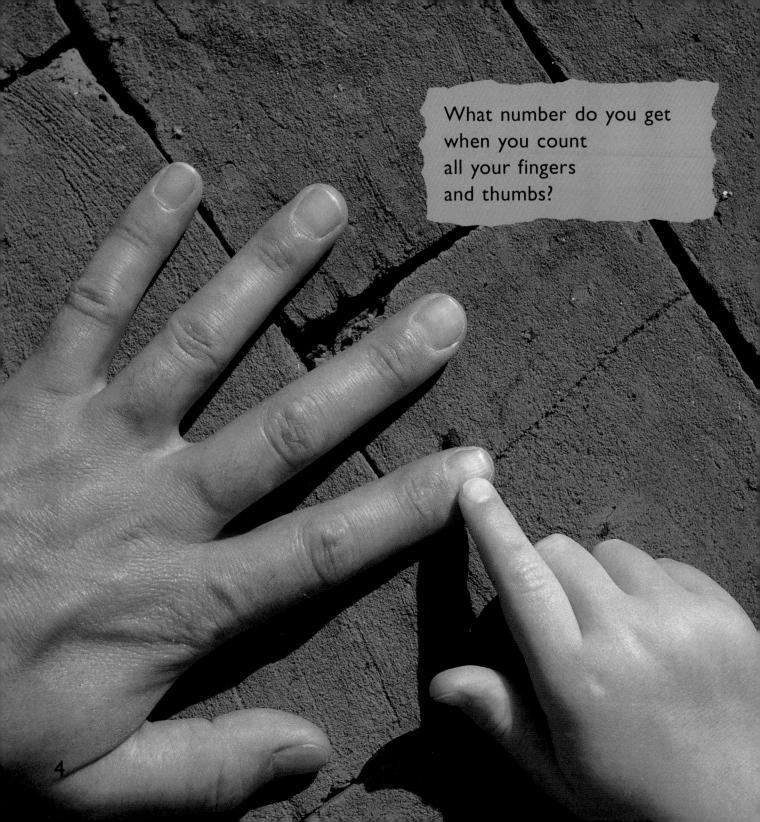

What number do you get
when you count
all your fingers
and thumbs?

4

Have you ever counted steps
as you go up and down?

5

Perhaps you learned to count while getting dressed. How many buttons are still undone?

Perhaps you learned to count by helping to set the table. How many people are going to eat here?

Counting helps us find out "how many?"
How many chairs are here?

Now count again.
How many chairs are here now?
What other things can you count?

Two shoes make a pair.
How many pairs of shoes
can you see here?
How many shoes can you see?

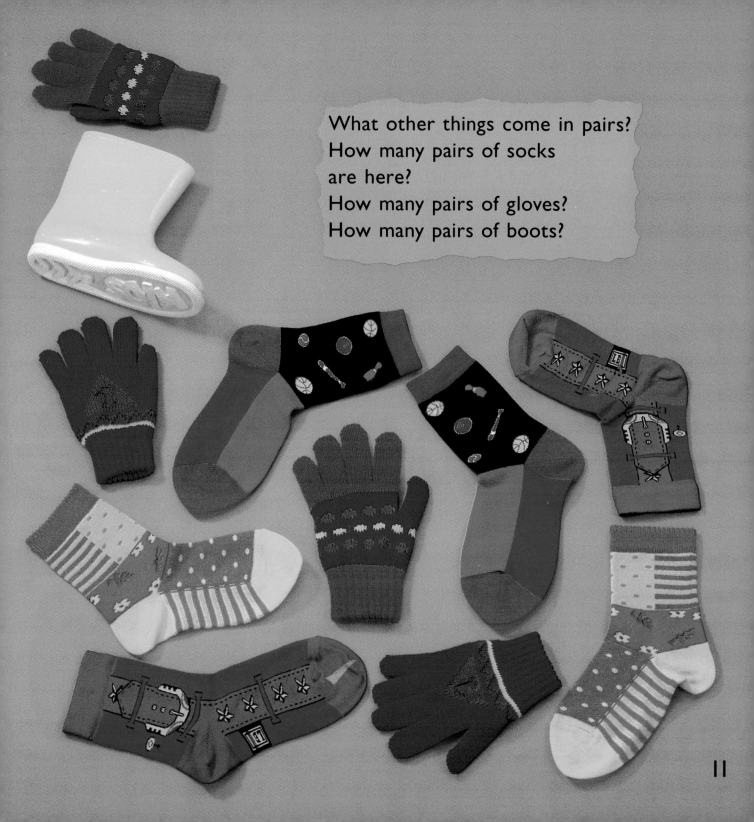

What other things come in pairs?
How many pairs of socks
are here?
How many pairs of gloves?
How many pairs of boots?

Each number has a shape
of its own.
How many of these numbers
do you know?

1 2

3 4 5 6

7 8 9 10

10

Can you place
these numbers in the
right order?

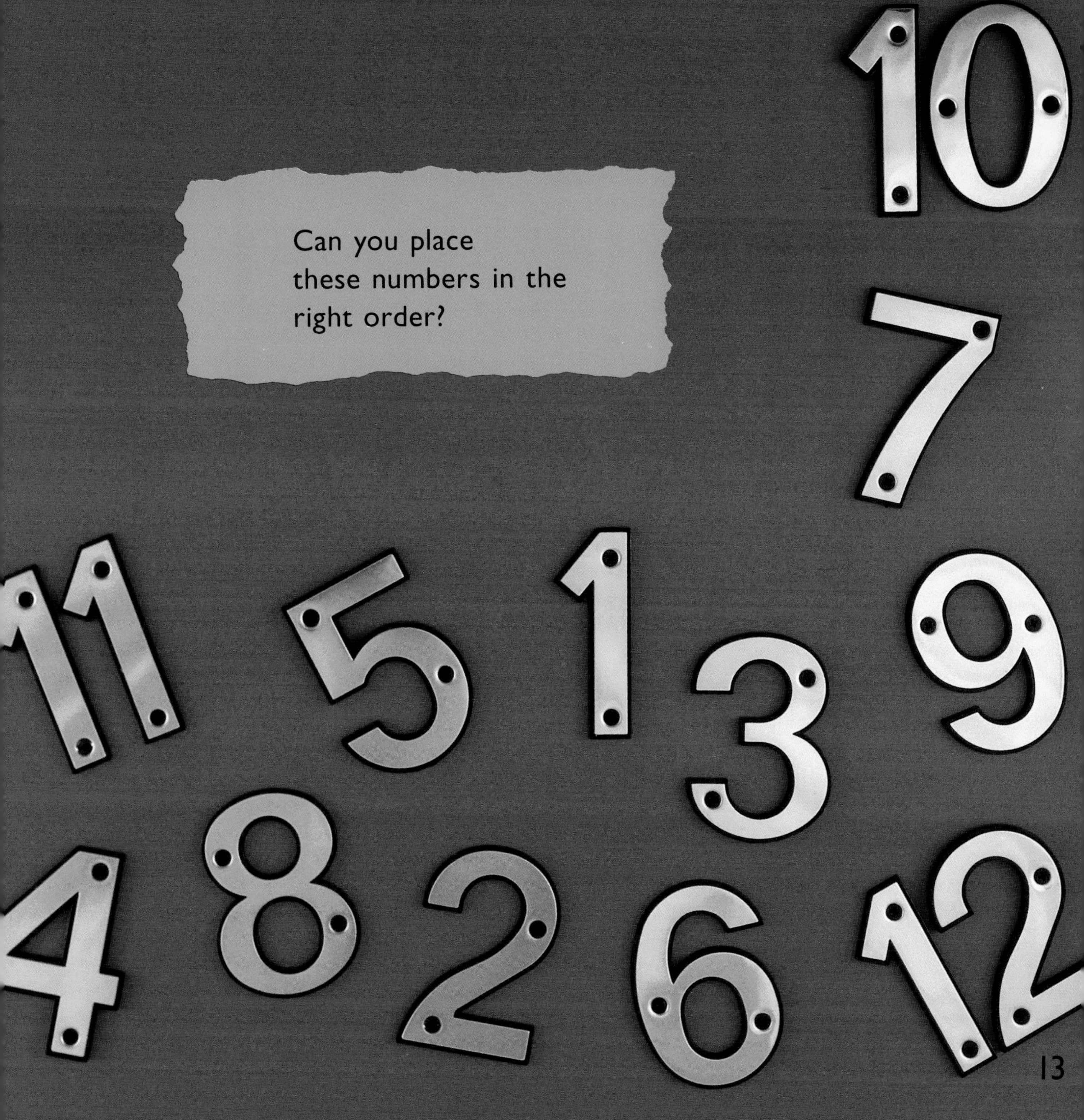

7

11

5

1

9

3

4

8

2

6

12

13

Collect some colored
buttons.
Make these patterns
with them.

Count each pattern.
How many buttons
are in each pattern?

Which pattern gives
an *even* number?

Which pattern gives
an *odd* number?

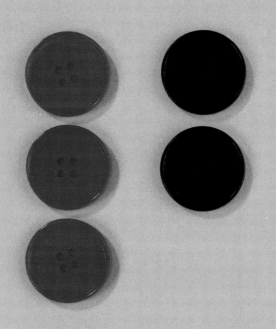
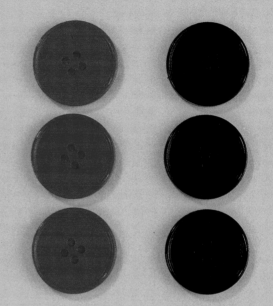
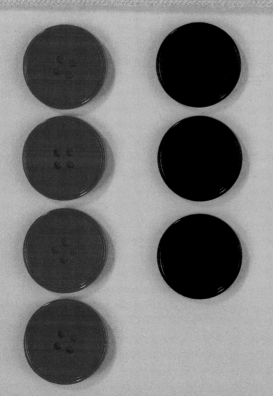

15

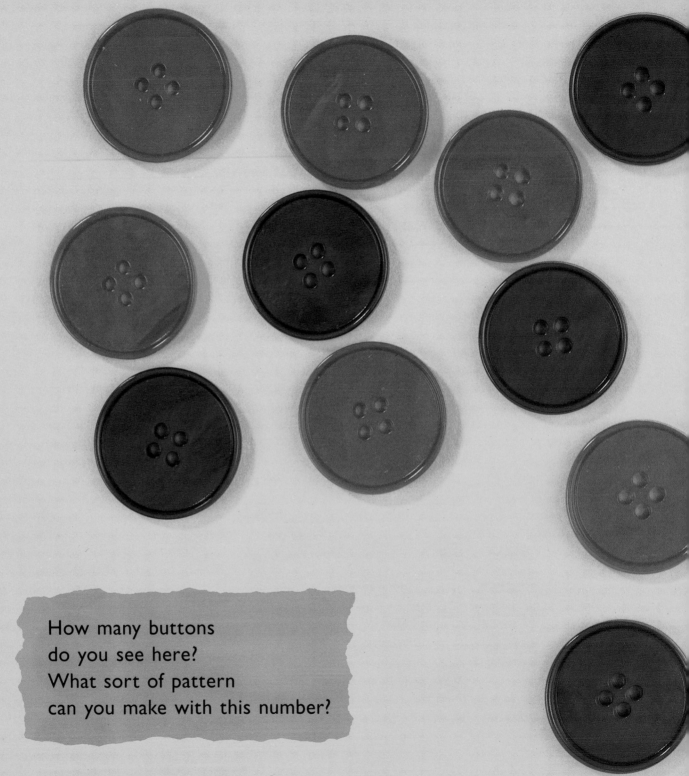

How many buttons
do you see here?
What sort of pattern
can you make with this number?

16

This page is empty.
What number do we use
to show there are
no buttons on this page?

How well can you count?
How many bricks
are in this pile?

How many shells
are on this sandy beach?

19

How many cows are in this picture? Count their legs.

How many toy people
are in this picture?
How many are standing?
How many are sitting?

21

Count these balls.
Are there fewer orange balls than white ones?

Which box contains more eggs?
How many eggs have been taken from each box?
How many eggs have been taken from both boxes?

We count to get
an exact answer
to the question
"How many?"
How many candies
have been eaten?

How many butterflies
are on these flowers?

It is very difficult to count
large numbers of things or people.
How many people are in this part of the crowd?

It is much easier to count the crowd as they line up to enter the stadium.

It is easier to count in ones and twos,

but scientists often have to use very large numbers in their work. How many stars can you count?

79

141

Do you know these large numbers?

46

55

How did you first learn to count?

Library of Congress Cataloging-in-Publication Data

Pluckrose, Henry Arthur.
    counting / Henry Pluckrose.
      p.   cm.
    Originally published: London; New York: F. Watts, 1988.
    (Math counts)
    Includes index.
    ISBN 0-516-45452-8
    1. Counting — Juvenile literature. [1. Counting.] I. Title.
QA133.P58   1995
513.2'11 — dc20   94-38012
                                                              CIP
                                                               AC

Photographic credits: Chris Fairclough 4, 6, 7, 8, 9, 10, 11, 12, 14, 15, 16, 17, 18, 19, 21, 22, 23, 24, 30; PhotoEdit © Michelle Bridwell, 5; Eye Ubiquitous © Davey Bold, 20; Bruce Coleman Ltd. © Dennis Green, 25; Unicorn Stock Photos © A. Gurmankin, 26, © Tommy Dodson, 31; Rex Features Ltd., 27; © Peter Millard, 28; Science Photo Library/Dennis Di Cicco, 29

Editor: Ruth Thomson
Design: Chloë Chessman

INDEX